INFLUENCING PEOPLE

ROY JOHNSON
& JOHN EATON

LONDON, NEW YORK, MUNICH,
MELBOURNE, AND DELHI

Senior Editor Jacky Jackson
Senior Art Editor Sarah Cowley
US Editors Margaret Parrish, Gary Werner
DTP Designer Rajen Shah
Production Controller Michelle Thomas

Managing Editor Adèle Hayward
Managing Art Editor Marianne Markham
Category Publisher Stephanie Jackson

Produced for Dorling Kindersley by

13 SOUTHGATE STREET WINCHESTER HAMPSHIRE SO23 9DZ

Designer Laura Watson
Editor Kate Hayward

First American Edition, 2002

02 03 04 05 10 9 8 7 6 5 4 3 2 1

Published in the United States by
DK Publishing, Inc., 375 Hudson Street
New York, NY 10014

Library of Congress Cataloging-in-Publication Data
Johnson, Roy, 1944-
    Influencing people / Roy Johnson & John Eaton
    p.cm.-- (Essential managers)
Includes index.
ISBN 0-7894-8950-3 (alk. paper)
    1. Organizational behavior. 2. Influence (Psychology) I. Eaton,
John, 1956- II. Title.
III. Series.

HD58.7 .J614 2002
658.4'5--dc21   2002019807

Reproduced by Colourscan, Singapore
Printed and bound in Hong Kong by Wing King Tong

See our complete product line at
www.dk.com

CONTENTS

4 INTRODUCTION

UNDERSTANDING INFLUENCE

6 BEING INFLUENTIAL

8 BUILDING COLLABORATION

10 THE PURPOSE OF INFLUENCE

MANAGING YOURSELF

14 BUILDING SELF-ASSURANCE

16 DEVELOPING INFLUENTIAL ATTITUDES

18 EMOTIONAL
INTELLIGENCE

20 DEVELOPING
EMPATHY

22 CREATING
TRUST

24 LOOKING
THE PART

PRESENTING
IDEAS

26 FRAMING
YOUR IDEAS

28 ENGAGING
INTEREST

30 GAINING
COOPERATION

32 SELLING YOUR
PROPOSAL

34 PROJECTING
THE FUTURE

EXERCISING
INFLUENCE

36 FORMING
NETWORKS

40 MOTIVATING
INDIVIDUALS

44 INFLUENCING
TEAMS

48 INFLUENCING
YOUR SUPERIORS

52 NEGOTIATING
SUCCESSFULLY

54 DISSOLVING
CONFLICT

58 REHEARSING A
PRESENTATION

62 SWAYING
AN AUDIENCE

66 ASSESSING YOUR
INFLUENCING SKILLS

70 INDEX

72 ACKNOWLEDGMENTS

INTRODUCTION

The ability to form mutually respectful relationships with others and to succeed in getting your ideas heard is a vital element of being a good manager. Having influence enables you to gain support and commitment for your proposals, and therefore increase your potential for success. Influencing People will help you build your communication skills, improve your ability to engage the interest and cooperation of others, and develop an authoritative and reliable reputation. Practical advice, including 101 concise tips, shows you how to develop influential attitudes and become someone to whom colleagues will look for advice and leadership. Finally, a self-assessment test at the end of the book enables you to evaluate your skills as an influencer.

UNDERSTANDING INFLUENCE

When you succeed in getting your ideas heard and accepted, you are exerting influence. Recognize that your powers of persuasion contribute directly to your ability to achieve your goals.

BEING INFLUENTIAL

Effective influencers are convincing and trustworthy, and both these qualities require self-management. In order to persuade others to accept your point of view, it is necessary to present a clear case that matches their needs.

1 Order your thoughts logically before you present an idea.

THE ART OF PERSUASION

Over 2,300 years ago, the Greek philosopher Aristotle summarized the skills required to become a successful influencer in his book on rhetoric. He defined persuasion as the ability to convince others to adopt your ideas. A good influencer is able to speak logically, fluently, and confidently. He or she is able to motivate and inspire others by appealing to their hidden interests.

◀ **THE ROOTS OF INFLUENCE**
Aristotle wrote that to be convincing, you need to learn how to win over minds with logic, to win over hearts with emotion, and to manage yourself so that you are seen as authoritative.

2 Study the techniques of public speakers.

3 Improve your credibility by being well-informed.

WINNING HEARTS AND MINDS

You win people's hearts when you respect their aspirations, interests, and concerns. In order to persuade people of the merits of a proposal, you will need to demonstrate how your ideas meet their needs, and let your enthusiasm for your ideas show, without letting it blind you to other people's views. In order to win minds, you must research your subject and present a good case. If someone has his or her own ideas, it will be necessary to negotiate a solution that meets their needs and yours.

MANAGING YOURSELF

Good influencers manage their emotions well. You can develop your confidence by noticing when you feel anxious, and then channeling this emotion in a positive way. For example, if you are nervous before a meeting, recall past successes and then imagine yourself doing well now.

Passionate

Logical

Adaptable

Honest

Fluent

HAVING INFLUENCE ▶
Effective influencers look and sound confident, well-rehearsed, and polished. They are alert to the feelings of others and adapt what they say accordingly.

CASE STUDY
Jan was a regional manager in an international organization. Her analytical approach to situations enabled her to win debates with her operating managers. However, she tended to call formal meetings to discuss issues, rather than having more informal 'chats'. Other staff found her unapproachable.
She began to notice that her colleague James was more influential within the company than she was, and consistently achieved better results. She realized that James spent time with his operating managers outside work hours and showed an interest in their personal values. The close relationships he built enabled him to exert influence and to reach agreements quickly.
Jan began to invest more time in her relationships with other managers and tried to understand their needs. Her ability to influence her colleagues began to improve.

◀ DEVELOPING INFLUENCE
In this case study, a manager found that she was not as successful as her colleague at forming agreements and achieving results. She watched to see how her colleague's techniques differed from her own and discovered how she could improve her influencing skills.

BUILDING COLLABORATION

All effective influencers cultivate collaboration with others and work to form productive relationships. Aim to be aware of people's needs and interests so that you can work together to reach mutually beneficial goals and solutions.

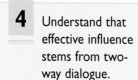

4 Understand that effective influence stems from two-way dialogue.

SEEING OTHER PEOPLE'S POINTS OF VIEW

Influence is not about forcing other people to accept your ideas – this would lead to resentment. It is about achieving the support of others to work toward mutually desirable goals. If you are in a discussion with a group, imagine yourself in their shoes: see, hear, and feel their response to your message. Adapt your ideas to their needs so that you will engage them more effectively. Seek their opinions before asking them to accept your ideas.

BEING ADAPTABLE

Prior to a one-to-one discussion, a meeting, or a presentation, make a list of the reasons why you think people will or will not go along with your ideas. Build these points into your communication, so that you appeal to the other party's motivations and preempt any objections. When you start talking, describe your goals in general terms and then ask your listeners what they feel is the most important consideration. Probe their views by asking questions. When you receive an answer to a question, give yourself time to reflect on it, and take it into account before you explain your idea in more detail. Adapt your ideas so that they incorporate the other party's views rather than persisting in your own proposals regardless.

5 Notice other people's body language when you suggest an idea.

6 Be flexible in your approach and consider the concerns of others.

QUESTIONS TO ASK YOURSELF

Q What do I want to achieve from this partnership?

Q What does my counterpart want from our relationship?

Q How can I dovetail these wants so that we are both happy?

Q What can I give up without sacrificing my overall goal?

Q What can my counterpart offer that may not be immediately obvious?

Q What new solutions serve our common goals?

FORMING PRODUCTIVE RELATIONSHIPS

Influence goes hand in hand with agreements. For example, in order to persuade someone to follow a course of action, you need to make agreements about what is to be done and by whom. Positional bargaining is where one side sets out a case and the other responds with a stronger argument in favor of his or her own position. Such competition leads to conflict in which the side with the most power wins and the loser resents the loss. Be creative and work to reach agreements that serve the interests of both parties, because this will be more beneficial in the long run.

WORKING EFFECTIVELY WITH OTHERS

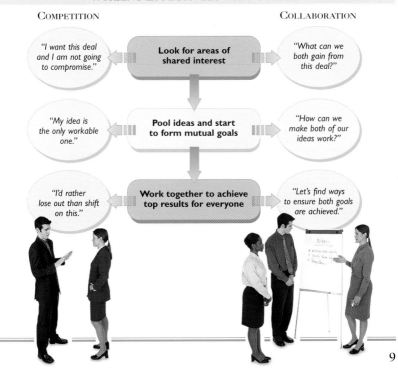

COMPETITION

"I want this deal and I am not going to compromise."

"My idea is the only workable one."

"I'd rather lose out than shift on this."

Look for areas of shared interest

Pool ideas and start to form mutual goals

Work together to achieve top results for everyone

COLLABORATION

"What can we both gain from this deal?"

"How can we make both of our ideas work?"

"Let's find ways to ensure both goals are achieved."

9

THE PURPOSE OF INFLUENCE

Good managers work with others to create agreements, build relationships, and achieve results. Be clear about what your goals are. Then, work with your senior managers, colleagues, and team to find shared interests and reach mutually desirable goals.

7 Understand how influence helps you create agreements with others.

INFLUENCING TO ACHIEVE A GOAL

Before you can satisfy mutual goals, you need to be clear about your own goals. This will help you focus your message. For example, before you introduce yourself to someone, think about what you want from the contact. If you want information, pinpoint what you want to know. If your goal is to interest others in your ideas, rehearse what you will say.

"SMART" GOALS

The mnemonic "SMART" will help you clarify your goals:
● Be *Specific* about what you want.
● Make sure that you can *Measure* results.
● Ensure that your goal is *Achievable*.
● Ask yourself if the goal is *Relevant*.
● Consider the *Timing* – by when does your goal need to be accomplished?

CREATING INTEREST

Manager matches relaxed approach of his superiors while he explains his ideas

Appeal to people by adapting what you say to their culture, needs, and attitudes. If you are addressing people junior to you, it may be necessary to take the lead; with superiors, you may only be required to deliver a brief. Before a discussion with someone, think about the approach you will take.

◀ ADAPTING STYLES
In this example, a manager matches the formal dress and informal manner of his senior managers so that they are more likely to react positively to his ideas.

REACHING AGREEMENTS

You can only get the support of others to help you achieve your goals by reaching agreements with them. Types of agreements may include customer service agreements or a joint resolve to cooperate on a project. Your ability to influence others will increase if you are able to be firm, yet flexible. Establish the interests you have in common with the other party and aim to meet their needs as well as your own.

8 Review and update your goals regularly.

▼ **FORMING AGREEMENTS**
Outline your proposals clearly and decisively, support them with evidence, and take into account the views of others.

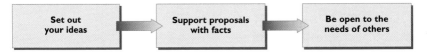

| Set out your ideas | Support proposals with facts | Be open to the needs of others |

UNDERSTANDING THE PURPOSES OF INFLUENCE

PURPOSE	METHODS
BUILD RELATIONSHIPS Create mutually beneficial relationships with others.	● Gain rapport. ● Dissolve fruitless conflict. ● Create mutual respect.
FORM AN AGREEMENT Agree on a solution that both parties are satisfied with.	● Ask questions to find out the other party's needs. ● Cooperate to find solutions that meet mutual goals. ● Incorporate other people's needs into your ideas.
WIN CUSTOMERS Put forward a proposal to a potentially new client.	● Work to understand the needs of your customers. ● Express your proposals with confidence. ● Present information that appeals to your listeners.
MOTIVATE TEAM MEMBERS Inspire team members to achieve top performance.	● Understand what drives each individual in your team. ● Outline the benefits for everyone involved in achieving team goals.
IMPROVE CAREER PROSPECTS Develop your career so that you can achieve your top potential.	● Understand your own ambitions and goals. ● Influence the senior managers in your organization. ● Build a network of useful contacts.

SWAYING OPINION

Research shows that opinions can be swayed by a variety of aspects, such as negotiation, debate, the presentation of facts, the credibility of the speaker, and the emotional appeal of the message. Combine as many of these methods as possible, adapting your message to suit whomever you are speaking to. In this way you can motivate individuals to achieve their goals; energize team members to work toward a common goal; get support for your ideas from your colleagues; or secure the backing of senior managers. To sway opinion in small groups or with individuals, make your message intimate and specific; to persuade larger groups, make your message more wide-ranging in scope.

STYLES OF SPEECH

After the battle of Gettysburg, Abraham Lincoln rekindled the morale of his men with a speech that began: "Four score and seven years ago, our fathers brought forth on this continent a new nation, conceived in liberty and dedicated to the proposition that all men are created equal...." His approach appealed to emotions and united his men in a common cause.

9 Win the respect and trust of your superiors.

10 Tailor your points to suit the decision makers.

INFLUENCING YOUR SENIOR MANAGERS

The first step to influencing senior managers is to develop your confidence in your ability to get your ideas across in a decisive way. You can do this by being clear about your goals. Take every opportunity to demonstrate to your senior managers that you can be trusted with challenges and authority. Exercise your powers of persuasion through maturity of judgment, a command of the issues, and the ability to put your ideas across clearly and dynamically.

DOS AND DON'TS

✔ Do identify the interests and concerns of those you wish to influence.

✔ Do be aware of other people's responses to your communication.

✘ Don't miss the clues that tell you that your approach is not working.

✘ Don't continue with a suggestion regardless of the affect you are having on others.

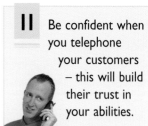

11 Be confident when you telephone your customers – this will build their trust in your abilities.

12 Consider what motivates you in your work.

 13 Make sure that you listen as well as speak.

INFLUENCING COLLEAGUES

Everyone has a good reason for being in their chosen occupation, whether this is a regular salary, convenient working hours, or the chance to be creative. Find out what motivates people, because the key to influence is knowing what people value. Ask your colleagues to think about how they could link their goals at work to their personal values so that they could increase their motivation levels. Then, link these values to your proposals so that you will be more likely to gain your colleagues' cooperation on a project.

INFLUENCING TEAMS

To build a top-performing team, you must first discover the shared values of your team members and outline a common purpose. This will prepare the way for the next influential step: to mobilize the shared energy of team members. Ask your team to consider how their inspirational goals could be achieved. Develop an action plan. While your team is working toward these goals, be available to defuse conflicts and motivate individuals.

MOTIVATING TEAMS

Establish the purpose of the team

↓

Identify and summarize immediate goals

↓

Discuss how these goals can be achieved

↓

Form a plan and allocate responsibilities

↓

Outline any goals for the future

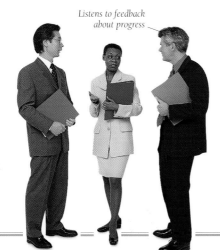

Listens to feedback about progress

◀ **BUILDING A TEAM**
When you are creating a project team, take the lead, brief the team well, and allocate responsibilities. Listen to feedback, and be available to offer advice and support as projects progress.

MANAGING YOURSELF

Good influencers look, sound, and act convincing. Take steps to increase your confidence, improve your ability to empathize with others, and build trusting relationships.

BUILDING SELF-ASSURANCE

People will place greater trust in your ideas if you communicate with confidence. Learn how to increase your poise and self-assurance, develop the ability to recover quickly from your mistakes, and build on your personal strengths.

14 Make it your goal to talk to new people wherever you go.

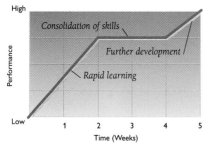

▲ **DEVELOPING SKILLS**
When you are improving performance, there is an initial period of rapid learning. Skills then need to be practiced before they improve further.

TAKING SMALL STEPS

If you are new to an organization or to the arts of influence, develop your confidence one step at a time. This will allow you to achieve each task you set yourself and reinforce what you learn. For example, approach colleagues from other departments and ask them to brief you on what is going on in their field. Begin to make more contributions. Speak up at meetings and work up to more ambitious presentations. Tolerate nervousness as the price you pay for progress.

MAINTAINING POISE

Relaxation is your most important aid, because when you are relaxed you can think clearly and respond to challenges. Learn to stay calm, whatever the situation, by practicing relaxation techniques until they become second nature. If you make mistakes, see them as learning opportunities. Detach yourself from the situation and ask, "What did I learn from that?" Learn to switch off negative self-talk such as, "I am no good at this."

Posture is upright and positive

15 Become a natural optimist – look for solutions rather than dwelling on problems.

▲ **BEING COMPOSED**
Always retain your composure so that you are better able to deal with any difficult situations that may arise.

BUILDING ON YOUR STRENGTHS

STRENGTH	DEVELOPMENT
ENERGETIC	Always be decisive when you outline your ideas to other people.
ORGANIZED	Make a point of planning your contributions to meetings or presentations meticulously.
FRIENDLY	Consistently put people at their ease with some well-chosen words, a compliment, or a smile.
KNOWLEDGEABLE	Keep up with current affairs and organizational matters, and subtly display your in-depth knowledge.
AMBITIOUS	Push yourself to take opportunities to lead meetings and make presentations to superiors and customers.
ANALYTICAL	Think through your ideas from every angle and consider every objection.

DEVELOPING INFLUENTIAL ATTITUDES

Effective influencers usually have a mission. They are motivated by their values and so they are able to lead others effectively. Identify your needs, hopes, and values, cultivate your leadership abilities, and start becoming more proactive.

16 Observe what good leaders do and aim to follow their lead.

FINDING YOUR MISSION

Take some time out to think about your talents, strengths, and long-term goals. What interests you most about your work? It could be writing, planning, or human relations among many other things. In the long run, you are more likely to be successful at your job if you are interested in what you are doing. Be clear and realistic about your limitations. Ask yourself what support you need from others and then set about getting it.

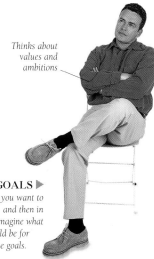

Thinks about values and ambitions

17 Ask a friend for feedback about your strengths, weaknesses, and abilities.

ANALYZING GOALS ▶
Think about where you want to be in a year's time, and then in five years' time. Imagine what your initial steps could be for achieving those goals.

DOS AND DON'TS

✔ Do believe in your abilities to achieve more in the future.

✔ Do welcome new challenges.

✔ Do continually strive to improve your skills.

✘ Don't feel defensive when others criticize your work.

✘ Don't shy away from more responsibility.

✘ Don't allow yourself to become complacent.

CULTIVATING LEADERSHIP

Leaders are people who can inspire others to participate in a vision. They are adept at balancing the need to get the job done with the need to maintain good relationships. The first step is to be clear about your purpose: this will give you an underlying strength that others will sense. The next step is to be clear about your organization's purpose. What needs to happen in order to overcome the obstacles to success? Once you have identified what needs to be done to achieve results, you are in a position to exert influence.

> **18** Decide what your first step toward leadership will be.

> **19** Understand that setbacks will happen.

Develop high expectations of yourself and others

Establish what is important for you and others to achieve

Define your intermediate and long-term goals

Harmonize your goals with your organization's goals

Gather ideas from others and get their support

Deliver a vision of the way things could be

Find ways to use others' strengths to achieve the vision

BECOMING PROACTIVE

To be an effective influencer, you need to do more than just wait for opportunities to come to you. Putting yourself at the forefront of projects that are going forward and taking every chance to make contacts is central to influence. People who back away from challenges are usually reactive – they see themselves as powerless to influence events. Become more proactive by acknowledging that you are responsible for what happens to you and always assume that life is what you make it. Interpret events in a positive way and take the initiative in making things happen. Learn from your mistakes and ignore situations that you cannot influence.

> **20** Recognize that influence comes from developing good relationships and sharing creative ideas.

◀ **DEVELOPING INFLUENCE**
Establish what you want to achieve personally and within your organization. Make your vision more realistic by defining how you and others can work together to build a successful future.

Emotional Intelligence

The ability to manage oneself and to build better relationships with others is vital for a successful influencer. Be aware of your own emotions, be sensitive to the feelings of others, and always act with honesty and openness.

21 Listen to your instincts when you are making difficult decisions.

Acting with Emotional Intelligence

The author Daniel Goldman states that you act with emotional intelligence when you are aware of, and regulate, your own emotions and when you are sensitive to the emotions of others. Get to know your own moods well. Pay attention to the emotional state of other people so that you can time your assertions sensitively.

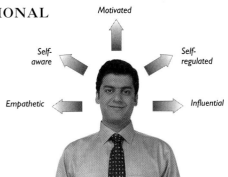

Motivated

Self-aware

Self-regulated

Empathetic

Influential

Points to Remember

- It is more productive to act with poise and determination, rather than to act out of fear or anger.
- By interpreting other people's nonverbal responses, you can gain insights about their feelings.
- Deal with other people's fears by exploring their assumptions.

22 Be aware of other people's preconceptions.

▲ EMOTIONALLY INTELLIGENT
An emotionally intelligent person understands his or her own strengths and weaknesses. He or she knows that it is more productive to manage emotions rather than be led by them.

Matching Behaviors

When people have rapport, they are mutually responsive. As one leans forward, the other will too; as one speaks slower, the other does too; when one relaxes, the response is mirrored. Build rapport by matching your counterpart's body language and voice tone. Then, to find out if you really do have rapport, subtly mismatch by leaning forward or speaking faster. If the other person copies you, it is a sign that you have good rapport and that the other party is open to your influence.

LEARNING TO READ NONVERBAL SIGNALS

Important clues to people's emotions can be found in nonverbal behaviors, such as gestures and facial expressions. By paying attention to these you can fine-tune your approach. Watch out for nonverbal signals that may indicate a person is drawing away from you. Look for behaviors that show you when someone is moving toward your view.

23 Match voice tones with others to build rapport.

▼ NOTICING SIGNS
Folded arms and a lack of eye contact indicate withdrawal. A positive expression and an open posture signal interest.

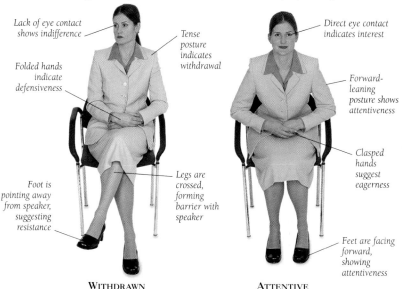

Lack of eye contact shows indifference

Tense posture indicates withdrawal

Folded hands indicate defensiveness

Foot is pointing away from speaker, suggesting resistance

Legs are crossed, forming barrier with speaker

WITHDRAWN

Direct eye contact indicates interest

Forward-leaning posture shows attentiveness

Clasped hands suggest eagerness

Feet are facing forward, showing attentiveness

ATTENTIVE

QUESTIONS TO ASK YOURSELF

Q How would I feel in that situation?

Q Am I being honest about my own feelings here?

Q Do I have a tendency to hide my own views on issues?

BEING OPEN WITH OTHERS

People are more likely to open up to those who act with sincerity. Be ready to share your emotions and values on a project and encourage openness in return. For example, if a colleague is discouraged by setbacks, speak about your own feelings of frustration in similar situations. Then explain how you overcame them.

DEVELOPING EMPATHY

Empathy is the ability to read a person's responses by imaginatively putting yourself in his or her place. Develop this skill by listening, and by asking questions that get to the root of concerns so that you can lead discussions in a positive way.

24 Try to interpret people's intentions, as well as listening to what they say.

BEING INTUITIVE

Gifted communicators have the ability to sense what others are thinking. When you are listening to someone, be intuitive. Use your imagination and your past experience of similar situations to give you some clues as to what the other person is feeling. Imagine that you are the other person and try to understand his or her needs.

◀ **INTERPRETING CAREFULLY**
Professional influencers, such as counselors, aim to understand the assumptions and needs behind what is being said so that they can start to solve issues.

GAUGING CONCERNS

When people tell you about something that is worrying them, they often talk around a subject instead of getting to the crux of the matter. If you feel that worries are not being aired, use questions that will help bring clues to the surface:

❝ *If you had the choice, what would you most like to happen now?* ❞

❝ *Can you give me five aspects that concern you about this issue?* ❞

❝ *What do you consider to be the fundamental thing that we should aim to achieve?* ❞

❝ *Are there any other issues that are worrying you about this situation?* ❞

LISTENING WITH "EARS"

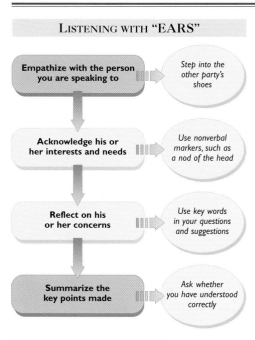

Empathize with the person you are speaking to → Step into the other party's shoes

Acknowledge his or her interests and needs → Use nonverbal markers, such as a nod of the head

Reflect on his or her concerns → Use key words in your questions and suggestions

Summarize the key points made → Ask whether you have understood correctly

ACTIVE LISTENING

Develop the art of structuring a conversation so that the other person feels heard, while you find out what is really at the heart of his or her concerns. Use the mnemonic "EARS" to help build rapport and understanding with another person, and to help you keep track of the key points being made. Listen for key words that express values, needs, hopes, goals, concerns, and interests.

25 Avoid giving advice unless you are asked for it.

QUESTIONS TO ASK YOURSELF

Q What assumptions are being made here?

Q Where else have I heard people voicing similar types of concerns?

Q Have I experienced a similar situation in the past?

Q What would it be like to be this person?

Q What else do I need to understand?

Q Is there something that I have missed, or have I gotten to the root of the issue here?

LEADING ON

Once you have developed empathy, you are in a position to lead a conversation in the direction you want to take it. Through empathy, you will have picked up some clues about the other person's thoughts and feelings. Having gathered this information, summarize what you have understood. Pause for a moment to check that your summary is accurate, then lead on with a question or a suggestion, such as, "Would it be useful to…?"

26 Check whether your intuitions are accurate by asking questions on the relevant points.

CREATING TRUST

People are more likely to be influenced by an individual they trust. Build a reputation for trustworthiness by speaking from a position of knowledge, keeping your promises, supporting others when they are in difficulty, and working through differences.

> **27** Remember that people respond well to honesty and courtesy.

Reads business sections every morning

▲ **KEEPING WELL-INFORMED**
Get to know as much as you can about your line of business. Read trade journals and keep up to date with current affairs.

DEVELOPING YOUR KNOWLEDGE

When you know your subject area well, others will pay attention to what you say. Knowledgeable people breed confidence. Recognize that the more answers you have to questions, the more people will come to you when they need advice. Knowledge on a smaller scale is also useful when you are holding meetings. Brief yourself thoroughly on every issue that is to be discussed. Be ready to take the lead in briefing others.

MEETING COMMITMENTS

People place trust in, and are influenced by, those they see as being reliable. People who do not keep their promises lose the trust of others quickly. Before you commit to new obligations, be sure that you can fulfill them. If you are not certain that you can, then say so; it is better to disappoint at this stage than later on. If, despite your best efforts, you are likely to miss a deadline, then call the other party and explain what has happened.

> **28** Say "no" to demands that may overstretch you.

▼ **BEING RELIABLE**
Before you agree to new obligations, check that you have enough time to do them and keep your promises.

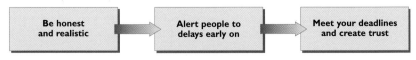

| Be honest and realistic | Alert people to delays early on | Meet your deadlines and create trust |

CREATING EMOTIONAL BANK BALANCES

An emotional bank balance in your favor arises when the "gifts" you have given a person outweigh the ones you have received. Such gifts may include help, advice, information, or support. They also include those signs of personal interest that are so well appreciated: remembered personal details, such as a family event or a partner's activities; a smile; a shared lunch; or a phone call. Offer support sooner rather than later – do not wait to be asked before offering it.

29 Keep a record of things that you have agreed to do and check it daily.

▼ **ANALYZING ATTITUDES**
Think about your behavior patterns at work – imagine how they influence the way your colleagues view you.

NEGATIVE ATTITUDE | POSITIVE ATTITUDE

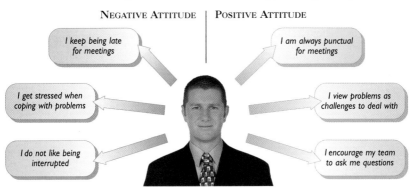

I keep being late for meetings

I am always punctual for meetings

I get stressed when coping with problems

I view problems as challenges to deal with

I do not like being interrupted

I encourage my team to ask me questions

THINGS TO DO

1. Be open about your wants and needs.
2. Make allowance for the weaknesses of others.
3. Acknowledge your own shortfalls.
4. Be quick to make amends for your mistakes.

WORKING THROUGH DIFFERENCES

If mistrust has arisen, bury the hatchet by first being open and honest about what has happened. Make amends for your own mistakes and ask what can be done to rectify them. Voice your own concerns sincerely and listen carefully to the concerns of the other party. Learn to tolerate and explore the reasons behind differences in opinions because opposing views can often spark the best and most creative ideas. Explore agreements, but allow for different points of view.

LOOKING THE PART

The way you present yourself in your dress and in your body language affects the way people perceive you and react to you. Make a good impression by dressing to match the business culture you work in and by emanating confidence.

> **30** Notice the way that successful people in your organization dress.

MAKING AN IMPACT

Research shows that people tend to form their first impressions within three minutes of meeting newcomers. They will be guided by dress, voice, handshake, grooming, and facial expressions. First impressions are very difficult to eradicate. In order to increase your influencing skills, notice the impact that you make on others.

◀ **CREATING THE RIGHT IMPRESSION**
If you take care with your appearance, you will create a favorable impression, and you will be seen as someone who is reliable and authoritative.

MATCHING THE CULTURE

Dress code in many businesses has undergone a quiet revolution. For example, the suit has been discarded in favor of informal wear in some industries. Adapt what you wear to match the organization in which you work, because the way you dress will affect how you are perceived by colleagues, superiors, and clients. Be ready to adapt to match the practices of customers too.

> **31** Find out a customer's dress code before a meeting and adapt your clothing to match.

WHAT TO WEAR

Codes of dress vary between businesses and industries as well as between countries. For example, established industries such as banking, accounting, and consultancy are generally more formal in their dress style – most staff wear suits. Meanwhile, design companies, publishing, and the media often favor a more casual approach to dress.

CREATING THE LOOK

Pick out your clothes carefully, because they will contribute to the impression that you make. For example, wearing a red shirt with a dark suit can make you feel more dynamic, while yellow can inspire mental stimulation. Neutral colors are very approachable and are particularly suitable if your job is very people-orientated. As well as taking care with your dress, focus on your body language too. Retain a relaxed, upright posture. Never slouch or lean on furniture. Relax your face muscles so that they are ready to break into a smile. When greeting people, ask how they are and be ready to inquire how their families are, too.

32 Allow enough time for grooming each morning.

33 Choose clothes that are well coordinated and stylish.

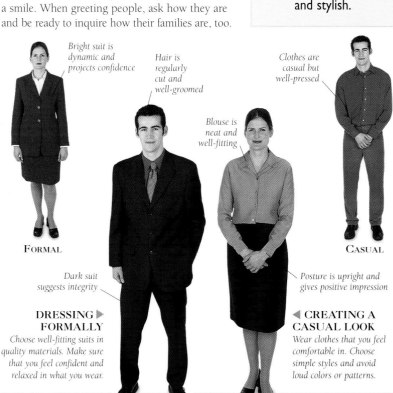

Bright suit is dynamic and projects confidence

Hair is regularly cut and well-groomed

Clothes are casual but well-pressed

Blouse is neat and well-fitting

FORMAL

CASUAL

Dark suit suggests integrity

Posture is upright and gives positive impression

DRESSING ▶ FORMALLY
Choose well-fitting suits in quality materials. Make sure that you feel confident and relaxed in what you wear.

◀ CREATING A CASUAL LOOK
Wear clothes that you feel comfortable in. Choose simple styles and avoid loud colors or patterns.

PRESENTING IDEAS

Your ability to persuade others rests on your ability to
present a well-argued, logical case backed by evidence. Make
your arguments attractive and engage your listener's interest.

FRAMING YOUR IDEAS

*In order to persuade someone to agree with
your point of view, your ideas should be
structured and well thought-out. Present
your proposals in a logical way and phrase
suggestions carefully so that you can guide
discussions effectively.*

> **34** Give your proposal
> a catchy name
> so that it grabs
> people's attention.

```
ENGAGE
Outline the benefits
        ↓
INFORM
Describe the facts
        ↓
EXPLAIN
Talk through the process
        ↓
PROJECT
Visualize the result
```

STRUCTURING YOUR IDEAS

People respond positively to proposals that are
well organized. Catch people's interest from the
start by letting them know why acting on your
proposals will benefit them. Then, describe the
underlying principles of your ideas so that the
basis for your proposals is clear. Show how your
idea will work in practice. Ask people to imagine
ways in which they could apply your ideas, too.

◀ **PRESENTING IDEAS LOGICALLY**
*Use this template to help you present ideas. You will soon find
that the method becomes automatic, and you will be able to order
your thoughts, even when you are speaking off-the-cuff.*

USING FRAMES

Give structure to discussions by putting a clear "frame" around your communication. For example, using a "goal frame" means that you specify what you want to achieve. The purpose of a frame is to let people know the intent behind your words and to focus people's thinking. Preface remarks with a simple statement of purpose, such as, "Let's turn our minds to solutions" (a "solution frame") or, "Let's see how many new ideas we can come up with" (an "idea frame").

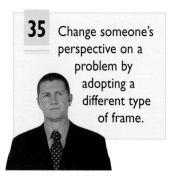

35 Change someone's perspective on a problem by adopting a different type of frame.

USEFUL FRAMES

TYPE OF FRAME	EXAMPLE
GOAL FRAME Specify what is wanted.	"Let's move on now and look at our goals." "What do we want to achieve?"
CREATIVE FRAME Generate ideas to solve a problem.	"Let's create a space for creative thinking." "This is the right time for a brainstorming session."
ACTION FRAME Set deadlines and allocate responsibilities.	"Now we've got some options open to us, let us look at who will do what and by when."
CRITICAL FRAME Identify pitfalls in a suggestion.	"Let's take a moment to consider the pitfalls of this proposal."

POINTS TO REMEMBER

- It can help you stay positive if you replace the word "but" with "and."
- A timely joke or an anecdote can often help change the frame.
- It is important to focus on positive issues, rather than being sidetracked by problems and negative points.

CHANGING THE FRAME

You can help people to see ways out of blind alleys by changing the frame they are currently in. Do this by finding another angle on the issue and then presenting it. For example, if people are bogged down in detail say, "Let's step back from the detail for a moment and consider the big picture." If someone is swamped by old problems, switch from a past to a future frame. Ask, "How will this need to be different a year from today?"

ENGAGING INTEREST

To influence people effectively, you need to find a connection between your goals and their needs and wishes. Find out what the other party wants, and use key words that emphasize these benefits as part of your proposals – draw your listener in.

> **36** Take the viewpoint of the person you want to influence.

ASSESSING BENEFITS

Describing how your idea, product, or service meets the needs of the people for whom it is intended is a powerful tool. Selling a fast car illustrates this idea. The fast car's powerful acceleration is a benefit for someone who enjoys driving quickly. But for a sedate driver, this confers no benefit at all. Identify your customers' needs, then focus on how they can benefit personally from the product or idea.

ANGLING YOUR SALES PITCH ▶
This car salesman recognizes that his customer is concerned about maintenance of the car, so he emphasizes this aspect in his sales pitch.

> **37** Notice what people are enthusiastic about.

> **38** Ask focused questions to help identify needs.

ESTABLISHING BENEFITS

The needs that people express in their own words have more credibility to them than the needs you tell them they have. For example, you may want to convince your manager to implement a new procedure. Ask him or her what he or she likes about the current methods. The answers you receive will tell you what needs to be preserved or improved by your proposal. Relate the new method specifically to your manager's needs. For example, if he or she likes the reliability of the current approach, emphasize this aspect in your proposal.

IDENTIFYING A HOOK

A hook is an aspect of your idea that meets the most important need of the listener – the key benefit. Use a hook to grab people's interest. In selling the new production method, for example, your manager's most important need may be increasing production rates to meet increased sales. So, your hook could be: "I want to propose a way to increase production and satisfy sales demands."

GAINING INSIGHTS ▶
If you want to influence a customer, it can help to gain as much background information as possible so that you can understand their values.

39 When you sell an idea, highlight the key benefits only.

KEY WORDS

To help you engage people's interest, choose words that make your ideas connect. Visual words include "notice," "bright," and "pinpoint." Auditory words include "click," "tune," and "resonate." Feeling words include "grab," "hunch," and "impress." For example, "Using my plan has *clear* benefits that are in *tune* with our strategy, and will have an *impact* on production."

MAKING A CONNECTION

Influential people create compelling images of the benefits their listeners will derive from the ideas they advocate. They let us know what we will see and hear, and how we will feel. You can do this by using words that create pictures, sounds, and feelings to make your ideas connect with the person you are talking to. So, for example, you could express the "hook" for the production improvement as follows: "I want to *show* (visual) you how we can *beef up* (feeling) production, *harmonize* with sales (sound), and relieve the *pressure* (feeling) on us all."

QUESTIONS TO ASK

Q What do you like about the current situation?

Q What would you like to change?

Q What is most important to you?

Q How can this be useful?

Q What do you need from this?

Q Do you have a particular preference for a course of action?

GAINING COOPERATION

Effective influencers are open and constructive communicators. Always strive to keep discussions objective and positive by taking care over the words you choose, focusing on the essentials, and creating a reputation for openness.

40 Use "we" rather than "you" when seeking the support of others.

41 Take a deep breath before you react to a criticism.

BEING POSITIVE ▼
Managers who phrase things positively, and who specify what benefits are in it for others, inspire action and loyalty.

STATING THE OUTCOME

When people know what you are asking for, it becomes easier for them to make a decision. This means making your requests in terms of what you do want rather than in terms of what you do not want. For example, instead of saying, "We never meet deadlines" say, "Let's get this done by December 31st." Remember that managers who continually state things in the negative are often thought of as moaners.

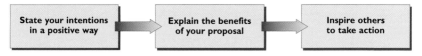

State your intentions in a positive way → Explain the benefits of your proposal → Inspire others to take action

EXPLAINING YOUR REASONS

Research shows that when people link their requests with a reason, they are much more likely to get a "yes" response. Try to phrase your requests carefully, so that you get the response you require:

❝ Will you let me chair the meeting? I have some announcements to make. ❞

❝ Would you finish the project by Friday? The customer made a special request for it. ❞

❝ Can you approve the report today? My team is eager to get started as soon as possible. ❞

❝ Can you meet with me soon? Then we can get the project moving. ❞

FOCUSING ON REASONS

When you put forward a proposal, choose one or two powerful arguments in your favor and concentrate on them. You risk diluting your case with weak arguments if you identify too many reasons. For example, you could come up with many reasons to convince your boss to allow you to work at home for a few days each month. Instead, choose two strong arguments to form a more convincing case. For example, point out that if you work at home, you will be able to clear twice as much work and will therefore have time to improve team performance.

QUESTIONS TO ASK YOURSELF

Q Am I usually able to direct a discussion toward a positive outcome?

Q Do I phrase things in a way that presupposes a successful result?

Q Do I emphasize words that indicate what I want to happen, or do I assume that other people will make the connections for themselves?

PRESENTING THE FULL PICTURE ▼

This manager is presenting an idea to her team. She is precise and specific about the problems that need to be overcome, but she also explains how it will be possible to deal with these. Her enthusiasm and positive attitude gain her the cooperation of her staff.

42 Bring contentious issues out into the open.

Colleague listens with interest

Manager explains how idea will work and conveys enthusiasm and commitment

Team member listens to ideas and asks questions

Handouts give details about proposal

SELLING YOUR PROPOSAL

When you are presenting an idea to another party, it is important to describe the steps by which the action plan will be accomplished. Explain how the process will work, and talk about what will be done to deal with any difficulties.

43 Keep the end goal in mind when you are explaining ideas.

44 Distribute handouts during a presentation – these should highlight your key points.

SPECIFYING THE PROCESS

Whatever your proposal, it needs to be accessible to the other party, whether this is one person or many. When you are explaining your ideas, keep to the point – you can hold another meeting or take questions by email once the other party has had a chance to think things through. Your main object at this stage is to show that your ideas are valid.

IDENTIFYING KEY INFLUENCE POINTS

PROPOSAL	EXAMPLE OF KEY INFLUENCE POINT
REALLOCATE ROLES	Explain how the new roles make the most of each team member's strengths.
DEVELOP NEW PRODUCTS	Talk about how the proposed products will effectively meet customers' needs.
CHANGE PROCEDURES	Explain how the new procedures will improve the effectiveness of administrative tasks.
INTRODUCE NEW SYSTEMS	Point out the benefits that new technologies will bring.
IMPLEMENT TRAINING	Show how training will reflect well on your organization's commitment to its staff.

BEING LOGICAL

When making your proposal, take your listeners step-by-step through to the final goal. Mention who will be involved, over what period of time, with what resources and support, and where the action will take place. You will come across as naturally influential when you demonstrate that you have thought things through. Show confidence in your ideas and handle objections with ease.

Asks valid question

Manager answers concisely

▲ OUTLINING PLANS

Describe exactly how a project will progress, detail any possible problems that will need to be handled, and answer any questions that arise. Your confident attitude will inspire trust in others.

45 Acknowledge the limits of your proposal.

46 Make your explanations as simple as possible.

QUESTIONS TO ASK YOURSELF

Q Would I invest money and time in this plan?

Q What is the worst thing that could happen?

Q Have I dealt with all my doubts?

Q Have I looked at the alternatives?

DESCRIBING CONTINGENCY PLANS

No plan can deal with every eventuality, but the more you anticipate, the more robust your ideas will become. Think about the likely obstacles and figure out how they can be dealt with. Look at your ideas from the point of view of your worst critic. Then revise your plans until you have taken into account every contingency. If there are problems you cannot solve, say so.

▼ BEING PREPARED FOR PROBLEMS

When you are proposing an idea, do not hide the potential risks involved in your suggestion. Highlight the possible problems, but then go on to explain how these can be dealt with.

Suggest ideas for dealing with potential problems

SOLUTIONS
● Plan response to unavoidable risk
● Allocate resources

Highlight possible obstacles

RISKS
● Predict potential problems
● Identify known risks and threats

PROJECTING THE FUTURE

Inspire individuals or teams so that they are motivated to achieve the goals you have set out. Engage the imagination of others by encouraging them to consider the practical, far-reaching, and exciting implications of your ideas and proposals.

> **47** Create a mental picture of a desired future to help make it happen.

PREDICTING SUCCESS

When you are proposing something to someone, describe a future that engages his or her imagination. Imagine changes to the individual's life that your proposals could make and then describe the pictures you see, the words you hear, and the feelings you experience from his or her standpoint. Demonstrate how the person will benefit personally from your ideas.

VISUALIZING SUCCESS ▶
The benefits of visualization are proven in the fields of sports and the performing arts. By imagining success, you can aim high and achieve your goals.

HANDLING OBJECTIONS WITH QUESTIONS

If someone makes an objection to your proposal, it can be useful to respond with a question. This will help you both look for solutions to problems, rather than being defeated by them. Use questions to encourage constructive thinking:

❝ *If you feel that we cannot afford the product, what can we do about the budget constraints?* ❞

❝ *If we cannot begin this project now, when would be a good time to start it?* ❞

❝ *If the proposal does not meet the requirements, what can be done to ensure that it does?* ❞

❝ *If you feel that the procedure is fine as it stands, can you outline what you like about the present approach?* ❞

IDENTIFYING SPIN-OFFS

Mention any knock-on effect your ideas will have on the team, the organization, the customers, and on the market. Think widely. These gains may seem marginal to you, but may be more central to the person you are addressing and so will sell your idea more effectively. Project a future in which your ideas are working and point out the ripple effects that they have. Engage the other person in this search for spin-offs.

48 Watch the other party's responses to your suggestions and, if necessary, change your approach.

POINTS TO REMEMBER

● If you keep your words general, your listener will have room for his or her own thoughts.

● Discuss the other party's responses with him or her and search for insights.

● It is helpful to use visual aids when you are presenting an idea, so that your listeners can picture results.

ELICITING POSITIVE RESPONSES

People will more readily commit to benefits they can see in their minds' eye. Encourage your listeners to envision outcomes for themselves. Assume that your ideas will be turned into action. For example, say, "When we have taken the first steps ....," rather than, "If we go ahead ..." Ask questions that induce your listeners to think through the application of your ideas.

ENCOURAGING POSITIVE ACTION BY ASSUMING SUCCESS

NEGATIVE		POSITIVE
"If we decide to go ahead with this proposal..."	**Present your project proposal to your team**	"When we put these ideas into action..."
"Maybe we'll encounter some problems..."	**Explain the process and ask for your team's input**	"We will solve problems as they arise..."
"Perhaps you would like to think about..."	**Encourage your team to imagine a completed project**	"After we have completed the project..."

EXERCISING INFLUENCE

Your success as a manager is dependent on the help and cooperation of others. Engage the support of your colleagues, team, and superiors, and fine-tune your influencing skills.

FORMING NETWORKS

Building a network of supporters, allies, and potential helpers is the key to successful influencing. Make it a life-long habit to form partnerships and cultivate alliances through a genuine interest in the people around you.

49 Be confident, relaxed, and curious about the people you meet.

50 Remember that junior staff are tomorrow's bosses.

51 Start networking today – pick up the telephone.

EXPLAINING NETWORKS

Networks are loosely organized connections between people who have interests in common. An internet chat room is an example of a network. Another example is a circle of friends and acquaintances who meet occasionally at social events. Although not all of them will know everyone present, most of them will know at least one other person there. However, a network could also be a list of names in an address book. Networking involves making contact with others for two purposes: because it is fun and because business alliances can come from it.

- Good networking skills come from a desire to be of service to others.
- If you do not enjoy networking, you are unlikely to do it well – do not force it.
- People are often more receptive and approachable when they are at a social occasion.

TAKING OPPORTUNITIES

Networking opportunities arise all around you, such as at lunch breaks or while you are waiting for an elevator or walking through another department. Take the time to introduce yourself to people and exchange small talk about things that are happening in the organization. More formal opportunities for meeting people include training sessions and briefings. On these occasions, make the effort to get to know people.

◄ CHANCE MEETINGS

When you are on your lunch break and you see someone you recognize from another department, go out of your way to strike up a conversation. This could be the start of a useful alliance.

52 Be open to opportunities and new friends.

INTRODUCING YOURSELF

The first golden rule is to time your entrance. Wait until people are between conversations, or pausing, before introducing yourself. If you are in a group, match what you say to what has just been said and, if at all possible, do so humorously. The second golden rule is to smile. If you are with one other person then say "hello" and give your name. Mention things you both have in common if you can, such as a mutual acquaintance.

Good listener

Perceptive

Collaborative

Friendly

Socially aware

▲ A SUCCESSFUL NETWORKER

This manager is an effective networker because she is able to establish mutual interests quickly, she puts people at their ease, and she finds opportunities to help others.

MAKING ALLIANCES

The secret of successful influence in the long term is to give more than you take. Even if your new acquaintances cannot help you now, they may be able to in the future and they may be able to introduce you to others who can help you, too. See if you have projects in common, contacts to exchange, or information to share.

INTRODUCING ASSOCIATES ▶
An excellent way to create goodwill is to introduce people to each other – this helps build alliances and shows that you are generous and supportive of others.

53 Get your name known by writing articles in journals.

54 Plan events – this is a good way to make contacts.

CREATING FOCUS GROUPS

You can start your own network by organizing a weekly get-together after work with like-minded people. This could be as an informal group or it could be one with a specific focus. Start off your group by identifying a theme that will interest as many people as possible and then contact people with that same interest.

▼ BEING PART OF A FOCUS GROUP
These managers work in different departments within the same organization, but they have agreed to meet regularly to share ideas and discuss new developments.

Sales manager talks about new customer

Product manager has some insights to offer

FOLLOWING UP

You should follow up an initial meeting with a new acquaintance as soon as possible. For example, send a short email to the person to say how pleased you were to meet him or her. Be organized and keep the contact details of everyone you meet. Make notes on their work and experiences, and identify mutual interests. If the opportunity arises, invite acquaintances to the social occasions you arrange. If your relationship with a person is more formal than this, look out for opportunities to brief him or her on business matters that may be of interest.

Sends article and comments to acquaintance

KEEPING IN CONTACT ▶

This manager has seen an article in a journal that he knows an acquaintance will be very interested in, so he writes a short note and sends the article to her.

55 Keep in regular contact with your acquaintances through emails, telephone calls, or cards.

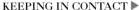

DOS AND DON'TS

☑ Do volunteer to lead new working groups.

☑ Do make a point of remembering names and personal details.

☑ Do be natural and open – insincerity is off-putting.

☑ Do be the first to initiate conversations at social meetings.

☑ Do be the first to offer help when others need it.

☒ Don't ask people intrusive questions about their work.

☒ Don't take refusals personally.

☒ Don't worry if progress is slow – be persistent.

☒ Don't talk about your own achievements instead of taking an interest in others.

☒ Don't forget that even senior directors are people just like you.

FILING DETAILS

As your lists of contacts and acquaintances grows, develop a filing system of their details. This should include address, telephone, and email details as well as any notes on correspondence. It can be useful to categorize your contacts under headings, such as the type of business they are involved in or their particular interests. Then, if you come across a useful article in a journal, for example, you can refer to your filing and quickly identify who would find the information useful.

MOTIVATING INDIVIDUALS

To achieve top performance from others, it is necessary to excite their interest in your ideas. Build trusting relationships with individuals, understand their values, involve them in decision making, secure their commitment, and give the necessary support.

56 Find out what interests team members have outside their work.

LAYING FOUNDATIONS

You are more likely to gain people's willing cooperation if you have a sound relationship with them. Look for opportunities to build mutual respect. Offer people support when they need it, and they will then be more likely to respond favorably to your requests for cooperation. When you talk to people, match their nonverbal behavior to build rapport. It will predispose them toward giving you a fair hearing.

Manager chats to his team about his weekend

▲ **BUILDING RELATIONSHIPS**
Invest time and care in your relationships with team members and colleagues. Meet for coffee breaks, get to know them on a personal level, and respond positively to requests for help.

57 Build confidence by focusing on people's strengths.

58 Keep your team informed about developments.

SETTING THE SCENE

Always aim to engage people's interest. For example, when you give a team member a new task or an additional responsibility, give the details of the whole project so that he or she feels involved. Knowing the big picture is motivating because people can see how they will contribute to an important outcome and this will inspire them to take an active part. Let individuals know how their contribution will affect team morale, customer loyalty, employee satisfaction, sales, profit, productivity, and so on.

ESTABLISHING MOTIVES

People are motivated to do what they like doing. They may not, however, be motivated to do what you want them to do. Discover people's values by asking them what is important to them. Then engage them by identifying how they gain personally from your plans. For example, if you know that your colleague values job security, emphasize how the new project means that there will be plenty of work for the year.

NOTICING VALUES ▶
A manager notices his employee's family photograph. He points out that if the proposal goes ahead, the employee will be able to work at home some days.

INVOLVING OTHERS

Participating in decision making motivates people. For example, when you talk to a colleague about how a job could be done, view it as an exercise in joint problem solving. If you have differing views, write them down. Then, brainstorm ways of closing the gap. Once you have agreed on a goal, work out how to achieve it: let your colleague influence the process, so that he or she will be as committed as you are to the outcome.

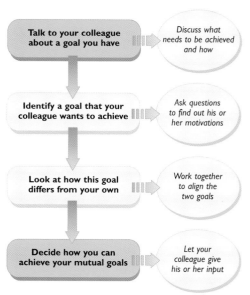

Talk to your colleague about a goal you have	Discuss what needs to be achieved and how
Identify a goal that your colleague wants to achieve	Ask questions to find out his or her motivations
Look at how this goal differs from your own	Work together to align the two goals
Decide how you can achieve your mutual goals	Let your colleague give his or her input

▲ MOTIVATING OTHERS
Discuss your mutual goals with team members and look at how these can be aligned. When people feel that their own input is valued, they will be better motivated to achieve results.

59 Motivate quieter team members by asking them for their ideas.

SECURING COMMITMENT

Cement people's interest by emphasizing what they stand to gain. To check commitment, use a closed question – one that calls for a definitive answer. For example, ask, "Do you feel happy about doing what we have agreed upon?" Look for a clear "yes" answer backed up by convincing nonverbal signs. If you see signs of doubt, work to resolve it. Ask a probing question such as, "What are your other thoughts about this?" and follow it with a question to find solutions, such as, "What do we need to do to enable you to resolve this?"

60 Look for signs of doubt, such as lack of eye contact.

61 If you cannot achieve a big goal, try a smaller one.

62 Be firm and fair when you assess others' ideas.

▼ **PROVIDING TRAINING**
To ensure the success of a new procedure, it is essential to arrange training so that people can develop the necessary skills.

ENSURING IT HAPPENS

As well as wanting to do a task, people need to know how to do it and also have the chance to do it. Give them the best chance of succeeding in a task by providing the necessary resources. This could include giving them the necessary authority, a budget, or administrative support. If time is an issue, work with them to change priorities, reassign tasks, and improve time management.

QUESTIONS TO ASK OTHERS

Q Have you considered what steps we could now take?

Q What options are open to us at this point?

Q What one thing could you do that would make a difference to this situation?

Q What possibilities have we still not tried yet?

Q Have we neglected any important aspects?

Q How soon can we get this project moving?

Q What procedures could we put in place to help us monitor this project?

63 Show enthusiasm when you brief someone – energy is contagious.

USING PUSH/PULL STYLE

The push style of influence involves telling someone what to do. The pull style involves asking questions that presume the other person will take the initiative. A push style is useful when a person's confidence and competence is low. People feel more secure if they are told what to do. Use a push style with inexperienced people and gradually move to a pull style as they develop.

▼ USING "PULL" INFLUENCE

A "pull" style of influence suits most occasions. Help your team members to take the initiative by asking them leading questions and motivating them to make their own decisions.

Manager asks team member for new ideas on project

CASE STUDY

Mark was a regional manager for an American financial company. He had been sent to work in the Brazilian office of his organization for a two year period. He found that his new manager interfered with his work and did not involve him in decisions. He also resented being so far away from his family. Mark's work began to suffer, and his manager confronted him about his performance.

Mark explained what he wanted from his job. He mentioned that he had been given latitude in decision making in his past job, and he also explained that he wanted to be able to spend some time with his family. His boss was sympathetic and agreed to broad parameters so that Mark could have more authority. His contract was changed to allow for a trip home twice a year. Mark's motivation levels began to improve dramatically.

◀ BEING MOTIVATED

In this example, a manager felt that his values and input were not being respected. His motivation levels fell. When he discussed his feelings with his manager, the issue was resolved and his motivation levels started to rise.

INFLUENCING TEAMS

The same principles that govern the means of influencing individuals apply to teams. However, you must also influence the relationship between team members. Define a team purpose, bring together diverse talents, and harmonize efforts.

64 Notice how the most influential person in a group is also the leader.

65 Exert influence by showing your expertise.

EXERCISING LEADERSHIP

Group dynamics are complex and can shift very quickly. If you are the manager of a team, you influence others through your authority. However, unless you back up your position with a vision for the team, and by concern for your relationship with team members, your influence may be undermined. If you are not the team manager, then you can exert influence through your experience and the trust you have won from others.

TAKING THE LEAD ▼
In this informal meeting, the best-informed member of the team naturally takes on the role of leader.

Business manager is impressed by what he hears

Sales administrator listens attentively to colleague

Manager is inspired by sales assistant's ideas

Sales assistant shows knowledge and leads discussion

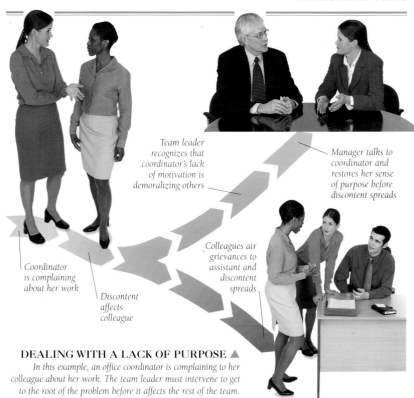

Team leader recognizes that coordinator's lack of motivation is demoralizing others

Manager talks to coordinator and restores her sense of purpose before discontent spreads

Colleagues air grievances to assistant and discontent spreads

Coordinator is complaining about her work

Discontent affects colleague

DEALING WITH A LACK OF PURPOSE ▲
In this example, an office coordinator is complaining to her colleague about her work. The team leader must intervene to get to the root of the problem before it affects the rest of the team.

CULTURAL DIFFERENCES

In some cultures, such as Japan, subordinates tend to be subservient to their team leader. In Western cultures, such as the United States, the style of leadership tends to be more democratic. Team members are encouraged to speak their minds.

SETTING AN EXAMPLE

The model of leadership you should offer is to some extent determined by the nature of the group you are working with. For example, a team that is not achieving results may need an authoritative figure who will set a clear direction. A successful team with many talented members may need a more democratic leader, while a team in conflict may need a leader who can reestablish good relationships. However, research shows that leaders who can combine all of these skills are likely to be most influential in the long run.

SETTING A JOINT PURPOSE

To influence people to work together as a team is not easy. Your best chance is to define a common purpose that everyone can believe in. This could be high standards, recognition of good work, a community ideal, or mutual growth. Whatever it is, it has to be something people are willing to give up their time and effort to have. Look carefully at the team's function – what is its purpose? What would it mean for it to do well? Then you will be in a position to outline these values to the team.

THINGS TO DO

1. Examine the function and strengths of the team.
2. Define the principle purpose of the team.
3. Outline this purpose to your team members.

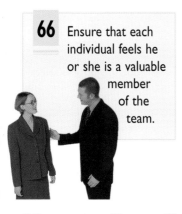

66 Ensure that each individual feels he or she is a valuable member of the team.

HANDLING DIVERSITY

Your team members may differ in their interests, needs, ages, motivations, and cultural backgrounds. Your job is to motivate them to work for themselves and for the team. Aim to create a climate of togetherness. Once you have defined the purposes of the team, establish how each member can contribute to it. Look hard at the strengths of each person and find a way that he or she could work to achieve the team's goals. Establish what each most wants to achieve and provide as many opportunities as possible for these goals to be achieved in return for teamwork.

HOLDING TEAM BRIEFINGS

In order to balance the team's capacity for creativity and criticism, you will need to set guidelines for team meetings. Having set the objective or the problem to be solved, ask for creative ideas that can meet the target. It is only after these ideas have been generated that you ask the group – together – to assess them. On this basis, the best alternative can be adopted and an action plan formed. Throughout this process, influence the team to focus on each phase of the meeting, rather than rushing to a solution.

67 Involve yourself in work your team dislikes.

68 Ask your team to suspend judgment and create ideas.

STEERING A DISCUSSION

A good question can bring the team's discussion alive in a way that advice never can. After you have summarized the key points made by the team, ask an open question that leads the discussion on in a positive way. By delaying making your contribution until this time, you will not inhibit your team from putting forward their own ideas. Have some good ideas to offer at this point.

DOS AND DON'TS

✔ Do be ready to take the lead.

✔ Do take time out to review teamwork.

✔ Do listen to your team first, before offering your own thoughts.

✘ Don't interfere if the team is working well.

✘ Don't hang on to projects that your team could do just as well.

✘ Don't create barriers within your team.

69 Build consensus by valuing everyone's input – encourage your team members to do the same.

▲ PLANNING ACTION
Influence your team's capacity for creativity and criticism. Direct discussions in a structured way so that you can work together to find solutions to problems and to form an action plan.

LEADING YOUR TEAM

A powerful way to direct a team discussion is to phrase things in a way that assumes something is about to happen. By subtly emphasizing the words that indicate what you want to happen, you can lead your team toward an agreement:

❝ *Before we decide on the solution, let's compare notes on what happened.* ❞

❝ *After we've discussed this, we can call the customer to let them know what we intend to do.* ❞

❝ *Have you had any good ideas yet on how we will handle this problem?* ❞

❝ *How easy will it be for you to finish this by next week?* ❞

INFLUENCING YOUR SUPERIORS

It is usually necessary to secure agreement from your superiors for your proposals. Demonstrate confidence and foresight, identify the criteria your managers will use to assess proposals, adapt your influencing style, and avoid forcing issues.

70 Build a reliable reputation so that your superiors learn to trust you.

71 Work to gain the respect of your superiors.

72 Imagine how you would react to your own proposals.

CREATING A REPUTATION

Work to impress your senior managers with your ability to handle responsibility. Ideally, you should already have had some success in seeing through high-profile projects to your credit. At the very least, build a reputation as someone who can be depended on to get results, troubleshoot problems, and spot opportunities. The better your track record, the more likely that your ideas will get a respectful hearing. Recognize that people are generally promoted when they have shown that they can work at the level above the one they are on currently – talk, think, and act accordingly.

ADAPTING YOUR IDEAS

The difference between superiors and their staff is that they have greater responsibilities. When influencing your superiors, consider their interests too – and adapt your proposals accordingly. Those in senior positions often need to take a long-term, large-scale view of an idea, such as how an idea will help the business grow. They will look beyond your ideas to assess their impact on the organization as a whole. Show that you have considered these matters also.

QUESTIONS TO ASK YOURSELF

Q Will my ideas make other people winners?

Q Is my presentation as brief as possible and have I assessed my ideas thoroughly?

Q Do I have an objective criteria for success?

Q Do my gut instincts support my plans?

Account manager notes concerns his directors have

Sales director asks about targets

Product director is interested in budget issues

Business director is focused on long-term

ASSESSING CRITERIA ▲
By listening to the types of questions that each of his senior managers asks about his proposal, this account manager can gauge their differing criteria.

73 Anticipate the criteria of each senior manager.

IDENTIFYING CRITERIA

Success in an organization comes from the collaboration of staff and the pooling of their various skills. Department managers all have varying special interests and concerns. For example, a financial manager will be principally concerned with accounting. However, he will also be involved in the long-term business development. Anticipate the criteria any given manager will use to evaluate your ideas, and adapt what you say accordingly.

MAKING YOUR MOVE

Once you have earned the right to be heard, studied your audience, and made your plans, it is time to make an informal approach. Timing is important: you are unlikely to get a good hearing if you approach others while they are overloaded with work. Mention that you have some ideas to share. Ask when the individual will be free to hear them, and then make an appointment.

CHOOSING A VENUE ▶
When you are introducing a proposal to a group, select a neutral venue. Arrange to meet everyone at the reception before proceeding to the meeting area.

ALIGNING PROPOSALS

Get interest in your proposals by establishing ways in which they meet the objectives of the organization, the department, or the team. Start by probing for agreement. State the outcomes you have in mind and then ask your senior managers whether they agree that these goals are important. Once you have commitment to the principles, go on to show how your plans will put them into action. This will work particularly well when you mention goals that you know are dear to the hearts and minds of the managers involved.

74 Be assertive about asking for the go-ahead.

75 Assume success – this will give you an air of confidence.

DOS AND DON'TS

✔ Do take the opportunity to mention your ideas at informal occasions.

✔ Do look for ways to show how acceptance of your proposals will reflect well on everyone involved.

✔ Do be your own best critic – this will give you confidence.

✘ Don't appear over-eager and don't show frustration or impatience.

✘ Don't throw away old proposals – they may come in useful another time in the future.

✘ Don't forget to have facts on hand – be prepared for any challenges.

CULTURAL DIFFERENCES

In cultures where management style tends to be democratic, leaders are more likely to accept feedback in a positive way. However, in status cultures, such as Italy, suggestions or criticisms given to managers in authority can be seen as disrespectful.

76 If someone objects to your proposal, ask for their ideas on how it could be improved.

OVERCOMING OBJECTIONS

Ask careful questions to establish what the objections are. Probe for the position behind the objections. Possibly the other party is confused or uncertain rather than antagonistic. If so, ask what needs to be established before the plan can go ahead. Look for ways to minimize risk, get support from others, reduce costs, and expand benefits. It is possible that your main proposal may be rejected. If so, then have a smaller proposal ready, which preserves at least some of your original ideas.

USING STYLES OF INFLUENCE

STYLE AND USE	METHOD
DEMONSTRATIVE To give an example of your idea successfully in action.	Outline examples of the same idea at work within the organization, or in another company.
TESTIMONIAL To show the listener that the idea has the support of others.	Provide testimonials of support from others or offer to present the idea to them.
CONSISTENT To show the listener that your proposal is in line with his or her principles.	Angle the proposal to show how it matches the needs of the listener.
TIME-AWARE To demonstrate how the plan will work in the long-run.	Offer to do a trial project, or to implement the plan in stages with regular reviews.
COST-FOCUSED To emphasize how costs and problems can be kept to a minimum.	Show how your approach resolves problems in a cost-effective way.

EXERCISING PATIENCE

A lack of interest may be visible in the nonverbal responses of your managers. If so, draw attention to this and ask for frankness in assessing your ideas. If your plans meet with criticism, do not take this personally. It is much more likely that the reasons for refusal are political and strategic rather than personal. If so, you may need to wait for the climate to change before trying again. If, despite your best efforts, you cannot gain any acceptance by reworking your proposal, then move on to something better. You will gain credit for your professionalism – and future presentations will meet with a better reception.

POINTS TO REMEMBER

● People are more likely to accept a smaller proposal if they have just rejected a larger one.

● You will lose respect if you do not heed feedback to your ideas.

● You should avoid being distracted by details, unless you are asked.

 77 Subtly match your superiors' nonverbal styles.

NEGOTIATING SUCCESSFULLY

It requires tact and diplomacy to handle negotiations well. Focus on interests rather than positions, prepare thoroughly, generate alternatives, remain composed when dealing with difficulties, and work to defuse disagreements.

78 Gain respect by addressing issues rather than winning arguments.

79 Take the time to think through proposals, rather than rushing to make a decision.

WORKING FROM PRINCIPLES

The classic approach to negotiation is for two sides to defend their own bargaining positions. However, if you win this battle of wills you may prejudice your relationship with your counterpart. Working from principles involves a more productive approach in which you are clear about your own needs and those of your counterpart. This will gain you more influence in the long run.

CASE STUDY

Sue, an account manager for a software development house, was called in to renegotiate a deal with a client. The buyer claimed that the cost of the product was in excess of what had originally been quoted.
    Before the meeting, Sue thought through the principles that were involved. She knew her company wanted to ensure a profitable relationship, and she guessed that the client wanted a fair deal.

During the meeting, Sue dealt with the initial anger of the disgruntled buyer, and then she laid out the principles as a potential basis for agreement. She also provided evidence that her organization's prices were competitive.
    Sue and the buyer agreed that the common principles underlying the deal were cost-effectiveness and a workable product. On this basis, they were then able to reach a satisfactory mutual agreement.

◀ NEGOTIATING EFFECTIVELY
In this case study, a manager was able to deal with a difficult negotiation by being clear about the underlying principles involved and using these as a basis from which they could form an agreement.

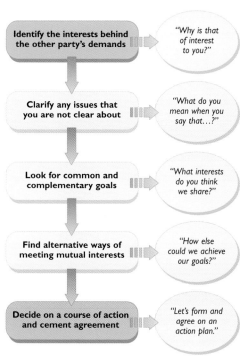

Identify the interests behind the other party's demands	"Why is that of interest to you?"
Clarify any issues that you are not clear about	"What do you mean when you say that...?"
Look for common and complementary goals	"What interests do you think we share?"
Find alternative ways of meeting mutual interests	"How else could we achieve our goals?"
Decide on a course of action and cement agreement	"Let's form and agree on an action plan."

◀ **FORMING AGREEMENT**
Use a step-by-step process of negotiation so that you can ensure that both parties are happy with the outcome.

NEGOTIATING

Identify what you want to gain from a negotiation and then predict your counterpart's goals. Ask your counterpart to clarify these. Collaborate to identify common goals and ways to achieve mutual goals. Then, come to an agreement and write a plan so that there can be no misunderstanding. This approach to negotiation enables both parties to achieve their goals.

80 Handle deadlocks by being firm but flexible.

COPING WITH OBSTRUCTION

Despite your best efforts at collaboration, the other party may become difficult or claim that the decision really rests with his or her managers. For example, the other party may say that if you do not give in, you will lose his or her support altogether. Refuse to be flustered and continue to press for information on facts, principles, and reasons. Avoid making concessions unless you are sure that you will get something tangible in return.

REMAINING CALM ▶
This manager remains composed, despite being faced with an irate customer. He presses for the facts of the case, and his positive attitude helps defuse the situation.

DISSOLVING CONFLICT

With the best intentions, arguments can escalate. Work to dissolve any conflict by acknowledging differences, validating other people's feelings, creating dialogue by referring to neutral criteria, and looking for areas on which you can agree.

81 Stay focused on your goals when you are faced with conflict.

NEUTRALIZING DISPUTES

Conflict can be creative if you can redirect it to find productive solutions and turn it into a platform for negotiation. If you find yourself involved in conflict, take a deep breath and focus your attention on the impersonal issues underlying the dispute. Ask a question that probes the cause of negative personal criticism, for example, "What makes you say that?" Outline the impersonal issues that you think are involved, and find out if the other person agrees.

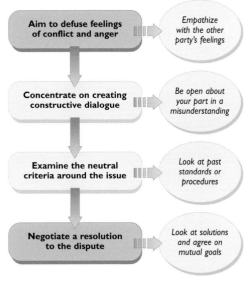

POINTS TO REMEMBER

● It is not necessary to agree with someone about every point.

● It is easy to spot the first signs of dispute by noticing nonverbal communication.

● If a discussion becomes too heated, it may be helpful to defer it to another day or move to more neutral territory.

▲ DEALING WITH A DISPUTE
When you are faced with a dispute, aim to defuse negative emotions quickly, so that you can begin to work toward a constructive resolution to the problem.

82 Find the cause of a problem and learn from your mistakes, rather than acting defensively.

VALIDATING PEOPLE

Often the emotion involved in a dispute can be discharged if you show you understand the other person's feelings. At the very least, the person will appreciate that you have listened. This does not mean that you should accept criticism even if you disagree with it. Make this distinction by focusing your comments on feelings. Say, "I understand that you are angry about this." Outline your interpretation of the other person's viewpoint to check that you understand and to reinforce the message that you are listening.

83 Respect diversity and everyone's right to disagree.

84 Remember that the best views are a synthesis of many.

SHOWING UNDERSTANDING ▼

In this example, this manager must act to defuse conflict by showing that she has understood all the different views, even when she does not necessarily agree with them.

Manager listens to both party's views and focuses her team on solutions

Team members get into a heated debate

Manager acts to defuse conflict

Manager fails to take control of situation and relations break down further

CREATING DIALOGUE

Once you have changed the focus of the dispute to less emotive matters, start a dialogue. The purpose of dialogue is mutual understanding: it assumes that there is no one right answer, and so it is the precursor to negotiation. Initiate dialogue by being open. If you see some way in which you may have contributed to the other person's anger, say so in a way that does not seem like a confession of guilt. For example, admit that you are sorry that a dispute has arisen and express your desire to bring the discussion back on track.

QUESTIONS TO ASK YOURSELF

Q Is there something that I have said in the past that may be at the root of this conflict?

Q Are there any areas where it may be possible to come to a mutual agreement?

Q Have I clarified the cause of my colleague's anger?

Q What alternative actions can I suggest at this point?

85 Learn from the way you dealt with past conflicts.

USING NEUTRAL CRITERIA

The use of neutral criteria enables you to move from dialogue to negotiation. Such criteria are based on precedence standards and are independent of the views of the protagonists. For example, you may resolve a quarrel about pay by referring to human resources guidelines. Frame the discussion by suggesting that you both look through the paperwork to help cast light on the disagreement. Once you have both looked at the facts, work together to reach an agreement.

◀ **PRESENTING THE FACTS**
In this example, a budgetary dispute is resolved when the marketing assistant finds and produces the necessary paperwork. The figures can then be checked.

MEDIATING CONFLICT

Friction between managers, teams, and even between departments is an all too common feature of corporate life. Destructive conflicts can erode the efficiency and morale of the whole organization. By stepping in to mediate between adversaries, you will be able to defuse anger and bitterness, and restore a common sense of purpose. Remember that the key to doing this rests in helping both parties be clear about what they want, and what they are prepared to give to the other party in return for it.

86 Focus on agreements and find solutions.

87 Examine the causes of a misunderstanding.

DEALING WITH DIFFERENT SOURCES OF CONFLICT

SOURCE OF CONFLICT	WHAT TO SAY
AGGRESSION	"Isn't there a better way to come to an agreement?"
DIFFERENT PERCEPTIONS	"I can see how that happened…"
GOSSIP	"I wonder what that's based on?"
DEFENSIVENESS	"Blame is unconstructive. Let us focus on solutions."
MISUNDERSTANDING	"What causes you to think that?"
WORRY	"How can we work together to resolve this?"
BEING UNDERMINED	"I'm sorry, you should have been consulted about that."
LACK OF TRUST	"Can we put our differences in the past?"
RESENTMENT	"How can we deal with that?"
OBSTACLES	"Let's focus on the things we can influence."

REHEARSING A PRESENTATION

The difference between great speakers and average ones often lies in their preparation. To sound convincing as well as natural, practice speaking with confidence, rehearse what you have to say in detail, and be ready to deal with potential objections.

88 Keep notes on any anecdotes you hear that you could use in your talks.

Be clear about what you want to say

⬇

Consider why you are qualified to speak on the subject

⬇

Make sure that what you say will relate to your organization

⬇

Be clear about your goals and prepare brief points

DECIDING TO SPEAK

Your decision to speak at a meeting may be spontaneous or planned. You may be asked to give a presentation, or the decision may be yours. Bear in mind that it is not necessary to say a lot to be influential; some of the noisiest people are the least influential. Before a talk, ask yourself why you are speaking on this subject. Perhaps you know your subject well, or perhaps you are the most senior person there and are expected to lead.

◀ **PREPARING TO SPEAK**
Before you speak at a meeting or a presentation, think through what you are going to say so that you will say it with confidence and clarity. Write things out point by point.

DOS AND DON'TS

✔ Do think about what is important about the issue.	✘ Don't let fear stop you from speaking up at meetings.
✔ Do consider what will appeal to your audience.	✘ Don't leave rehearsals until the last minute – make sure that you are properly prepared.
✔ Do outline the benefits that will follow if people act on your proposals.	✘ Don't forget to include jokes and anecdotes in a presentation.

89 Think about people who present talks well and try to emulate them.

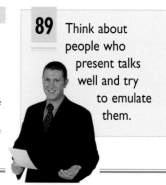

SPEAKING WITH CONFIDENCE

There are a number of techniques you can learn that will help you speak with conviction and project yourself confidently. If you have prepared a talk, always practice it beforehand. Pretend that you are addressing someone who is standing at the back of the room you are in. Put enthusiasm into your voice so that you will engage your audience, particularly at the start and finish. Try lowering your voice tone to demonstrate confidence – breathe deeply and start the sound of your voice in your chest, rather than in your throat. Vary your pace: slow down to make important points, and speed up to convey enthusiasm. Vary your volume: speaking quietly can make people sit up and listen, whereas a louder voice tone can be useful for making important points.

◀ REHEARSING A TALK
Try practicing a speech in front of a mirror so that you can take note of your body language, and make any necessary adjustments.

EXPLOITING PAST SUCCESSES

To get yourself into a positive state prior to your presentation, recall your past achievements in similar situations. If you have made successful presentations before, then recall the positive feeling you had at the time. Link this feeling to a trigger, such as a word or an image, so that imagining this word or image will automatically reproduce the positive feeling. If you have not made a presentation before, then remember a successful social occasion instead. Work on making a confident state second nature to you.

QUESTIONS TO ASK YOURSELF

Q When have I given a successful presentation in the past?

Q How did I feel at the beginning and at the end of my latest presentation?

Q In what way was that occasion similar to the present situation?

Q Are there any tactics that I used in the past presentation that I could draw on for this occasion?

90 Prepare your presentation well in advance.

91 Use positive self-talk to increase your confidence.

GETTING SUPPORT

Before a talk, ask people who will be there what their interests are, and adapt the content of your presentation accordingly. If any of the people you speak to are key decision makers, so much the better. Having prepared what you have to say, rehearse your presentation in front of someone else. Ask your adviser to be frank with you. Do not confuse any feedback you get with criticism. Try taping your presentation beforehand and playing it back to yourself. Notice how you could adjust your tone of voice or speed of delivery.

USING YOUR IMAGINATION

Make a presentation come alive in your own mind before you deliver it. Imagine that you are at the end of a successful meeting – what did you do that made it go well? Make a note of these success factors and be sure to include these during your presentation. When imagining the outcome, focus on what you will be seeing, hearing, and feeling as evidence of your success.

THINGS TO DO

1. Imagine how you will feel if your current presentation is a success.
2. Remain focused on these feelings of success.
3. Use these imagined positive feelings to increase your current confidence levels.

Manager feels happy and positive at end of her talk

◀ IMAGINING SUCCESS
Before a presentation, imagine yourself having just given a good talk, and picture the response of your audience.

Audience members appreciate good talk

ANTICIPATING OBJECTIONS

Even the best arguments meet with criticisms. To prepare for this, take on the role of your own worst critic and pick holes in your arguments. Write down your answers to the objections. An alternative course is to imagine that you are one of the influential people who will be present in your audience. What might this person say? Mentally rehearse your response to the "worst that could happen" so that you are confident you can handle anything.

▲ **BEING WELL PREPARED**
If you are well briefed and have carried out thorough research before a presentation, you will be able to deal with difficult questions or criticisms with ease.

DOS AND DON'TS

✔ Do read up on your subject thoroughly and be well-informed.

✔ Do use graphics to emphasize your key points and ideas.

✘ Don't let the thought of objections undermine your confidence.

✘ Don't be distracted from the main points that you want to make.

92 Arrive at a talk with plenty of time to prepare your materials.

CASE STUDY

Vanessa had been asked to present a key project to a party of customers. She began to prepare her material, but as the presentation drew nearer, she became increasingly nervous.. Unfortunately, during both her past presentations she had "frozen." She feared this would happen again.

She decided to work with a coach to remedy the problem. The coach helped her discover that the "freeze" response was triggered when she focused on the eyes of people in the audience. She learned instead to focus on the sound of her own voice and on a neutral spot on the back wall.

The coach helped her set up a positive state of confidence that could be triggered by the word "calm," which she could use if she froze. However, Vanessa found that because she was well prepared, she felt naturally confident. Her talk was a great success.

◀ **COPING WITH DIFFICULTIES**
In this example, a project manager was asked to prepare a presentation for a customer. By learning to deal with her nerves and by preparing herself for any difficulties she might encounter, she was able to deliver a successful presentation.

SWAYING AN AUDIENCE

The way you present an idea can make or break it. Inspire and persuade people with a lively style and expressive body language. Outline your key ideas, state how your proposals will be achieved, and handle interruptions with confidence.

93 Be ready to adapt your talk to match your audience's response.

MANAGING YOUR STATE OF MIND

Once you have rehearsed, prepared your materials, and tested any equipment you will be using, begin to get into the right frame of mind for your talk. Your state needs to be confident, relaxed, and energetic. Stand for a few moments on the spot where you will be delivering your talk. Try to visualize yourself taking charge of the room and the people who will occupy it.

94 Stand in the room where you will give your presentation and think of it as your own office.

THINGS TO DO

1. Create a positive, confident mental state.

2. Prepare a hook, such as an anecdote, that will help to draw your audience in.

3. Focus on the key words that your audience will be interested in, and make sure that you are ready to emphasize these points.

4. Decide how you will vary your tone of voice.

POINTS TO REMEMBER

● Even when you have prepared a talk thoroughly, always be ready to make adaptations depending on your audience's reaction.

● During a talk, breathe deeply and concentrate on staying relaxed.

● Watch out for loss of interest, and be ready to move on.

● Break up long presentations with activities or discussion groups.

INSPIRING AN AUDIENCE

Grab your audience's interest by starting with an appealing anecdote, quote, or story. Popular television programs, celebrities, and admired figures are a rich source of stories and quotes. So are any related problems, challenges, and rewards you have experienced. Telling an amusing story (if you have one) will also get the audience on your side. But then, move quickly on to tell your listeners what your talk is about and the benefits you want them to get from it.

ENLIVENING THE PRESENTATION

If you are presenting to a group, make your presentation as visually rich as you can. Well-designed slides and flip charts are helpful. One good image or diagram can often get an idea across better than a few hundred words. Use plenty of colors when you draw images or write bullet points. Use anecdotes to give examples for the points you are making and, wherever possible, think of a slogan to unite your material into a common theme.

Manager selects slides to use at her presentation

PREPARING VISUAL AIDS ▶
Invest the time in preparing visual aids for a presentation – slides can be a particularly effective way of keeping an audience interested in a talk.

95 Start by outlining the content of your talk.

96 Use bullet points to summarize your key points.

OUTLINING THE KEY IDEAS

There is a natural limit to the amount of information your audience can take in and remember after the event. For maximum impact, keep detail and complexity to the bare minimum. Summarize your key points and repeat these two or three times – preferably at the start and at the end of your talk. It is helpful to use an overhead projector so that your key points are visible throughout your talk. Provide direction to your listeners by telling them what the subject is, what problems it solves, and what the solution is.

CULTURAL DIFFERENCES

In the United States, public speakers often adopt an emotive style of speech. The language used is often fast-paced, and it is designed to make listeners feel personally involved in events.

In Western Europe, however, the style of public speaking is often more factually based and low-key. In the UK, speakers often use self-directed humor to break the ice and defuse tension.

97 State that you will answer questions at the end.

98 Change to a more upbeat tone when describing solutions.

CHOREOGRAPHING A TALK

It is not just what you say but the way that you say it that gets results. For example, when you stand with your weight on one foot, you come across as indecisive. However, when you stand with an upright and relaxed stance, with feet shoulder-width apart, you create an impression of confidence. Use your hands expressively to support your words, rather than simply waving them around. Move purposefully and try to present positive and negative points in different ways.

▼ USING YOUR BODY LANGUAGE
During a presentation, adapt your position and your posture as necessary. For example, when you outline a problem, stand behind the podium. Move forward to emphasize positive points.

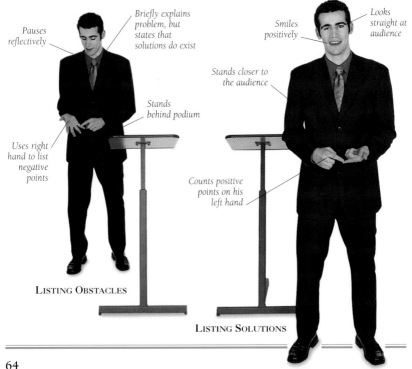

Pauses reflectively

Briefly explains problem, but states that solutions do exist

Smiles positively

Looks straight at audience

Stands closer to the audience

Stands behind podium

Uses right hand to list negative points

Counts positive points on his left hand

LISTING OBSTACLES

LISTING SOLUTIONS

99 Be ready for a range of questions about your proposal.

KEEPING IT SIMPLE ▼
A useful way to structure a presentation is to describe the present situation, say what you want to happen, and explain how.

STATING YOUR PRESENT POSITION

Be clear, precise, and specific about the problems to be overcome. The aim here is to provide feedback on what is happening now and what needs to be improved. Support what you say with facts and be ready to answer questions. If you are describing a new technique or process then talk about the problems it was designed to solve. Be positive in what you say and stress that the problems described do have a remedy.

| Explain your present position | → | Highlight your desired goal | → | Outline the resources required |

STATING THE SOLUTION

As quickly as possible, move on from talking about present issues or problems and say what you propose to do about the matter. Your solution could incorporate a change in procedure, a new technique, an organizational change, a proposal to a customer, a promotion, a reallocation of responsibility, a new product, or a call for more resources. Be sure to state clearly what your proposal will do and the goal you intend to achieve. Make sure that you define your ideas clearly and unambiguously.

100 Respond to interruptions positively.

101 Maintain the flow of your presentation.

POINTS TO REMEMBER

● Many objections contain ideas that can improve your proposal.
● Take persistent critics to one side at the end of the meeting and ask them for their suggestions.
● Always keep your cool, no matter what the provocation – your poise will work in your favor.

HANDLING INTERRUPTIONS

Interruptions can make a presentation come alive if handled in the right way. Listen to the speaker's comments politely. Check your understanding by summarizing it in your own words. Highlight points of agreement and answer the question. If you cannot answer, then promise to get back to the speaker later. If an interruption is aggressive, ask the rest of the audience if they have other views.

ASSESSING YOUR INFLUENCING SKILLS

Evaluate your powers of persuasion by responding to the following statements and marking the option closest to your experience. Be as honest as you can: if your answer is "never," circle Option 1; if it is "always," circle Option 4, and so on. Add your scores together, and refer to the Analysis to see how well you scored. Use your answers to identify the areas that need most improvement.

OPTIONS
1 Never
2 Occasionally
3 Frequently
4 Always

1 I look at other people's points of view before defining proposals.

1 2 3 4

3 I always express my ideas with confidence and enthusiasm.

1 2 3 4

5 I know my own strengths at work and use them to the fullest.

1 2 3 4

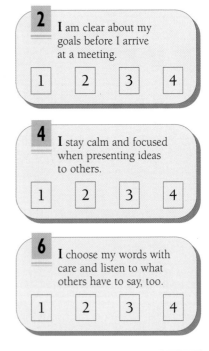

2 I am clear about my goals before I arrive at a meeting.

1 2 3 4

4 I stay calm and focused when presenting ideas to others.

1 2 3 4

6 I choose my words with care and listen to what others have to say, too.

1 2 3 4

7 I treat setbacks as learning opportunities, rather than problems.

| 1 | 2 | 3 | 4 |

8 I ensure that I am dressed appropriately, whatever the occasion.

| 1 | 2 | 3 | 4 |

9 I listen carefully to opposing views before summarizing them.

| 1 | 2 | 3 | 4 |

10 I am proactive and always looking for new opportunities.

| 1 | 2 | 3 | 4 |

11 I keep abreast of developments within my industry.

| 1 | 2 | 3 | 4 |

12 I take the first step in introducing myself to new acquaintances.

| 1 | 2 | 3 | 4 |

13 I back up my ideas with reasons and hard evidence.

| 1 | 2 | 3 | 4 |

14 I seek the support of senior managers for my goals and plans.

| 1 | 2 | 3 | 4 |

15 I acknowledge the needs, interests, and values of others.

| 1 | 2 | 3 | 4 |

16 I rehearse my presentations thoroughly beforehand.

| 1 | 2 | 3 | 4 |

17 I always keep my commitments and promises faithfully.

1   2   3   4

18 I handle conflicts by looking for and identifying mutual interests.

1   2   3   4

19 I use my voice and hands to emphasize suggestions.

1   2   3   4

20 I offer support and help to others without waiting to be asked.

1   2   3   4

21 I work through differences with others openly and honestly.

1   2   3   4

22 I listen for, and use, the emotive words used by the people I talk to.

1   2   3   4

23 I make my proposals attractive by explaining their benefits.

1   2   3   4

24 I balance the big picture with the broad detail so that everything is clear.

1   2   3   4

25 I neutralize disputes by trying to understand the other party's position.

1   2   3   4

26 I am comfortable working with people who are more senior than myself.

1   2   3   4

27 I assume that there can be a positive outcome to every issue.

| 1 | 2 | 3 | 4 |

28 I am specific about asking for what I want and the support I need.

| 1 | 2 | 3 | 4 |

29 I find out what matters to the people I work with.

| 1 | 2 | 3 | 4 |

30 I test for positive responses at every step of my proposals.

| 1 | 2 | 3 | 4 |

31 I regularly mix with new people and build my contacts.

| 1 | 2 | 3 | 4 |

32 I recognize my strengths and weaknesses and always work to improve my skills.

| 1 | 2 | 3 | 4 |

ANALYSIS

Now that you have completed the self-assessment, add up the scores and check your performance by referring to the evaluation below. Identify your weakest areas, and refer to the relevant sections in this book to hone your influencing skills.

32–63: You could be more influential. Focus on being proactive rather than reactive. Concentrate on finding common ground with others so that your self-presentation skills can start to develop.

64–95: You are influencing well and have built some good working relationships. However, expand your sphere of influence by winning over the hearts and minds of those around you.

96–128: You are a skilled influencer who relates to others well. Keep improving your abilities on your way to the top.

INDEX

A

action frames, presenting ideas, 27
action plans, 13
active listening, 21
adaptability, 8
agreements:
    productive relationships, 9
    types of, 11
alliances, networking, 38
anecdotes, giving a presentation, 62, 63
anticipating objections, rehearsing presentations, 61
appearance, personal, 24–25, 64
arguments, dissolving conflict, 54–57
Aristotle, 6
attitudes, analyzing, 23
audiences, swaying, 62–65

B

bargaining, positional, 9
behavior:
    analyzing attitudes, 23
    body language, 18–19, 40
    matching behaviors, 18
benefits, engaging interest, 28–29
body language:
    matching behaviors, 18
    personal appearance, 25
    presentations, 64
    reading nonverbal signals, 18–19, 40
briefing teams, 46

C

closed questions, securing commitment, 42
clothes, personal appearance, 24–25
cooperation, 30–31, 40
collaboration, 8–9
colleagues, influencing, 13
colors, choosing clothes, 25
commitment, 22, 42
communication:
    developing empathy, 20–21
    dissolving conflict, 54–57
    engaging interest, 28–29
    framing ideas, 27
confidence:
    building self-assurance, 7, 14–15
    creating trust, 22–23
    influencing senior managers, 12
    rehearsing presentations, 59
conflicts, 54–57
consistent style, 51
contingency plans, 33
conversations, leading, 21
cost-focused style, 51
creative frames, presenting ideas, 27
critical frames, presenting ideas, 27
cultural differences:
    influencing senior managers, 50
    leadership, 45
    presentations, 63

D

decision making, and motivation, 41
democratic cultures, influencing superiors, 50
demonstrative style, 51
dialogue, dissolving conflict, 56
discussions, steering, 47
disputes, 54–57
dress codes, 24

E

emails, networking, 39
"EARS," active listening, 21
emotions:
    dissolving conflict, 55
    emotional bank balance, 23
    emotional intelligence, 18–19
    managing your own, 7
    winning hearts and minds, 6, 7
empathy, 20–21
    dissolving conflict, 55
engaging interest, 28–29
eye contact, 19

F

facial expressions, 19
filing systems, networking, 39
first impressions, personal
    appearance, 24
focus groups, networking, 38
framing ideas, 26–27
future, projecting, 34–35

G

gestures, 19, 64
goal frames, presenting ideas, 27
goals:
    clarifying, 10
    finding your mission, 16
    influencing colleagues, 13
    influencing teams, 13, 46
    and motivation, 41
    negotiation, 53
    stating outcomes, 30
Goldman, Daniel, 18
group dynamics, influencing teams, 44

H

hooks, engaging interest, 29

I

ideas:
    framing, 26–27
    engaging interest in, 28–29
    giving a presentation, 63
    presenting ideas, 26–35
    selling proposals, 32–33
influence, purpose of, 10–13
intelligence, emotional, 18–19
interest, engaging, 28–29
interruptions, giving a presentation, 65
introductions, networking, 37
intuitive listening, 20

J

joint purpose, influencing teams, 46

K

key ideas, giving a presentation, 63
key words, engaging interest, 29
knowledge, creating trust, 22

L

language:
    engaging interest, 29

left-brain dominance, 16–17
Leonardo da Vinci, 33
logic:
    left-brain dominance, 16–17
    thought processes, 8

M

managerial time, 21
meetings, teams, 47, 48–51
men, mixed gender teams, 42
mental processes, 11, 16–17
Metaphor Analysis, 54
mind:
    exercising, 25
    subconscious mind, 30, 32
    unfreezing your mind, 32, 37
    see also brain; thought processes
mind mapping, 29, 37
monitoring action, 41
"must" criteria, 39

N

needs:
    clarifying, 38
    recognizing, 38
negative conditions, 33, 37
nonverbal behavior, "helicopter"
    approach, 30

O

open-ended problems, 23, 34
    brainstorming, 50, 52–3
    problem statements, 35
open-ended questions, 55, 56
operational time, 21
outcomes see goals

P

passive behavior, 55
patterns, breaking, 13
personal problems, 35
physical activity, 29, 37
planning:
    action plans, 40
    strategic time, 21
presentations, "Four Ps", 39
"Prime Model," 40
problems:
    brainstorming, 50, 52–53
    close-ended and open-ended,
        23, 34–35
    data dumping, 51
    "Five Whys" process, 31, 37, 38
    managing, 41
    mind mapping, 29, 37
    negative conditions, 33, 37

operational time, 21
problem statements, 35
reframing, 39
understanding contexts, 35
procedures, improving, 60–61
process reengineering, 60–61
professional problems, 35
professionals, outside help, 42–43

Q

questioning:
    asking questions, 55–57
    creative thinking, 7

R

Realist, Disney Strategy, 58–59
recruitment agencies, 43
reengineering, 60–61
reframing, 39
reviewing:
    ideas, 58–59
    performance, 65
    procedures, 60–61
ridicule, ignoring, 23
right-brain dominance, 16–17
"rounds," teamwork, 59
routines, "doing things
    differently," 32, 37

S

schedules, 21
selling ideas, 39
skills, team development, 64
sleep, subconscious mind, 32
social conditioning, 10
"soft" objectives, 41
solutions:
    "best fit" solutions, 20
    convergent thinking, 8
    divergent thinking, 9
    understanding contexts, 35
sport, 29, 37
statements, of problem, 35
stimulating creativity, 28–31
stimulating ideas, 54–57
strategic time, 21
subconscious mind, 30, 32
success, measuring, 41
SWOT analysis, 63

T

tasks, allocating, 40
teams, 44–65
    briefing, 47, 48
    constructive debate, 45
    cooperation, 44

creative processes, 48–51
Disney Strategy, 58–59
evaluating ideas, 62–63
improving effectiveness, 64–65
leading, 47, 49
mixed gender teams, 42
stimulating ideas, 54–7
"rounds," 59
setting up, 46–47
thinking see thought processes
third party problems, 35
thought processes, 11
    adapting, 20
    changing, 32–33
    convergent thinking, 8
    divergent thinking, 9, 20
    imagination, 13
    left and right brain, 16–17
    thinking patterns, 14–15
    thinking styles, 25
    types of thinkers, 58–59
    see also brain; mind
time management, 21
tools:
    creative approach, 36–37, 45
    reviewing processes, 60–61

U

unfreezing your mind, 32, 37
United States, cultural differences,
    49, 60

V

value reengineering, 60–61
visual images, 33, 37
visualizing outcomes, 35, 37

W

"want" criteria, 39
winners, recognizing, 50
women, mixed gender teams, 52
workplace conditioning, 10

ACKNOWLEDGMENTS

AUTHORS' ACKNOWLEDGMENTS

This book owes its existence to the vision and advice of Adèle Hayward and Jacky Jackson at Dorling Kindersley. We are particularly grateful for the enthusiastic way in which Kate Hayward and Laura Watson at Studio Cactus took up the challenge of turning the manuscript into a finished product. We owe much to the many inspiring writers on communication on whose work we have drawn and to the many managers and staff with whom we have worked who have helped us to turn ideas into practical techniques. We are indebted to Yvonne Eaton and Jane Slemeck for their support and many cogent lessons in influence.

PUBLISHER'S ACKNOWLEDGMENTS

Dorling Kindersley would like to thank the following for their help and participation:

Jacket Designers Brendan Kersey, Katy Wall; **Jacket Editor** Jane Oliver-Jedrzejak; **Indexer** Hilary Bird; **Proofreader** Polly Boyd; **Photography** Gary Ombler

Models Roger André, Phillip Argent, Carolyn Boult, Ed Burns, Angela Cameron, Kuo Kang Chen, Russell Cosh, Carol Evans, Vosjava Fahkro, John Gillard, Ben Glickman, Kate Hayward, Richard Hill, Cornell John, James Kearns, Zahid Malik, Brian Monaghan, Chantal Newall, Mary-Jane Robinson, Kiran Shah, Lynne Staff, Kerry O'Sullivan, Suki Tan, Gilbert Wu, Wendy Yun; **Make-up** Nicky Clarke

Picture research by Ilumi; **Picture librarian** Melanie Simmonds

PICTURE CREDITS

The publisher would like to thank the following for their kind permission to reproduce their photographs:

Key: *a*=above; *b*=bottom; *c*=center; *l*=left; *r*=right; *t*=top

Allsport: 34; **AKG:** Eric Lessing 6; **Corbis Stock Market:** Ariel Skelley 4/5; Charles Gupton 42; **Imagebank:** Barros & Barros 20; **Stone:** Stuart Hughs 24; David Young-Wolff 28; **Telegraph Colour Library:** John Terence Turner 37*c*; VCL 49*b*; Rob Brimson 61; **Jacket photography** © Eyewire and Dorling Kindersley

All other images © Dorling Kindersley
For further information see: www.dkimages.com

AUTHORS' BIOGRAPHIES

Roy Johnson, MBA, is a founder and director of Coaching Solutions and is also Director of Pace – an award-winning management training company with a wide variety of small- to large multinational clients. He is the author of *40 Activities for Training in NLP,* and coauthor with John Eaton of *Business Applications of NLP: 30 Activities for Training, Essential Managers: Coaching Successfully,* and *Communicate with Emotional Intelligence.* He and John Eaton have an on-line coaching skills training service on www.coachskills.com

Dr. John Eaton, PhD, is a founder and director of Coaching Solutions, an innovative company offering executive coaching and training programs in coaching skills to blue-chip companies throughout the UK. He contributes regularly to such journals as *Theory and Psychology, Organisations and People,* and *Changes and Training Journal.* He is also, with Roy Johnson, the author of *Business Applications of NLP: 30 Activities for Training, Essential Managers: Coaching Successfully,* and *Communicate with Emotional Intelligence.*